Thank you for taking the time to look at my book and there are Other

Helen's Hat Shop

The Hat go to the Derby

The Hat Vacation at the Dude Ranch

The art Hat's and Miss.

Witch Hat

No part of this book may be Reproduced or stored in a retrieval system or transmitted by any mean without the written permission of the author.
Published by Creative Space
6/30/2016

ISBN -13 – 978- 1977735911
ISBN- 10 - 197735916
library of congress # 2013909690

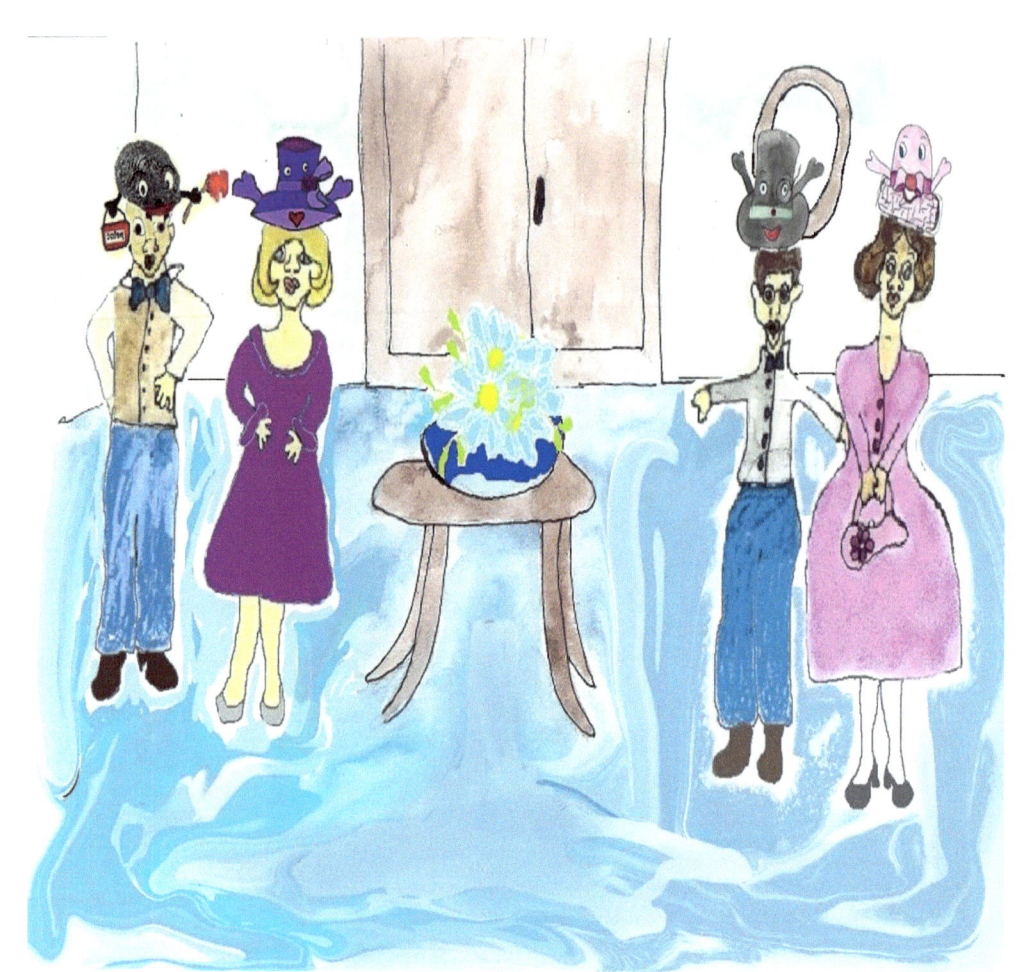

IT was the day of the Fifty Anniversary for the Old Town Library Mrs. Hubbard and her Family had their Hat on and out the door they went to the car

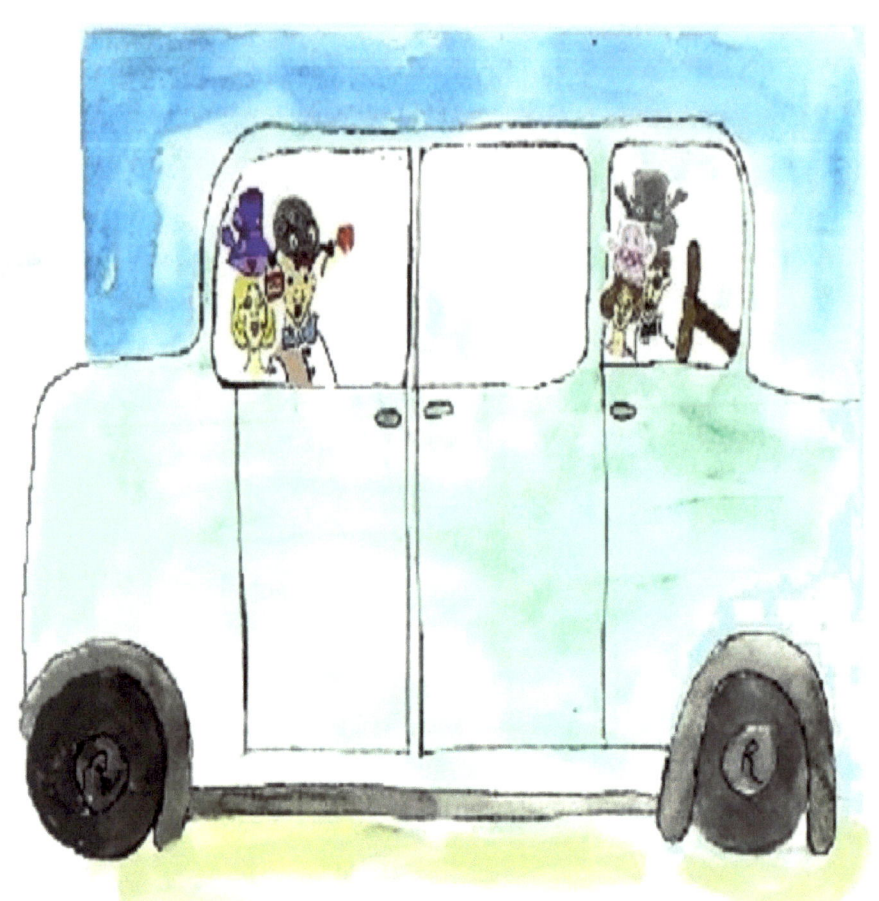

They had to go by Helen's Shop to pick her up for the party and go by Jim to get him it was a nice day for the Anniversary

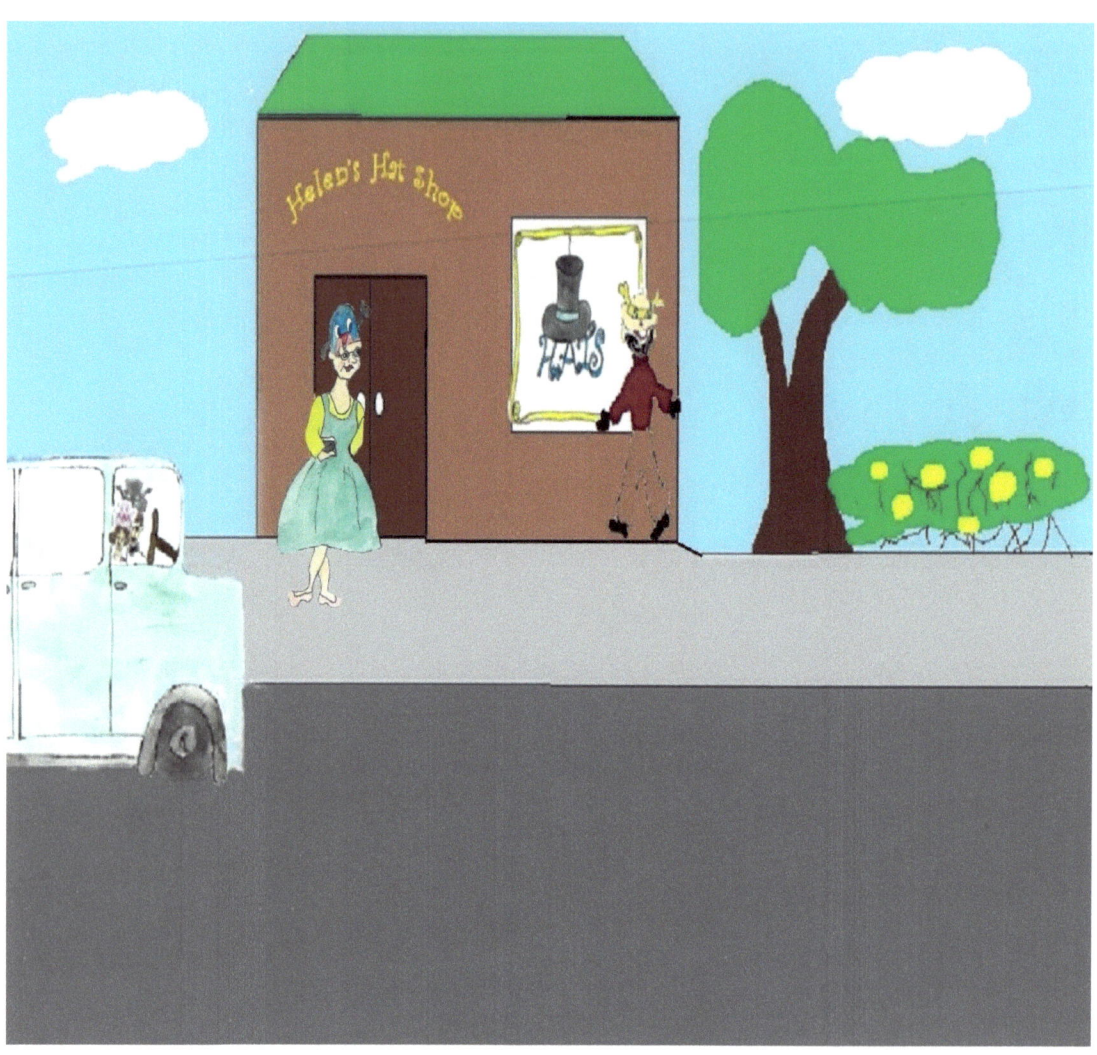

Helen's and Jim where waiting out front they hope in the front seat of the car there was room because Mr. Hubbard and Ms. Hubbard where in the front set that made room in the back for the four of them

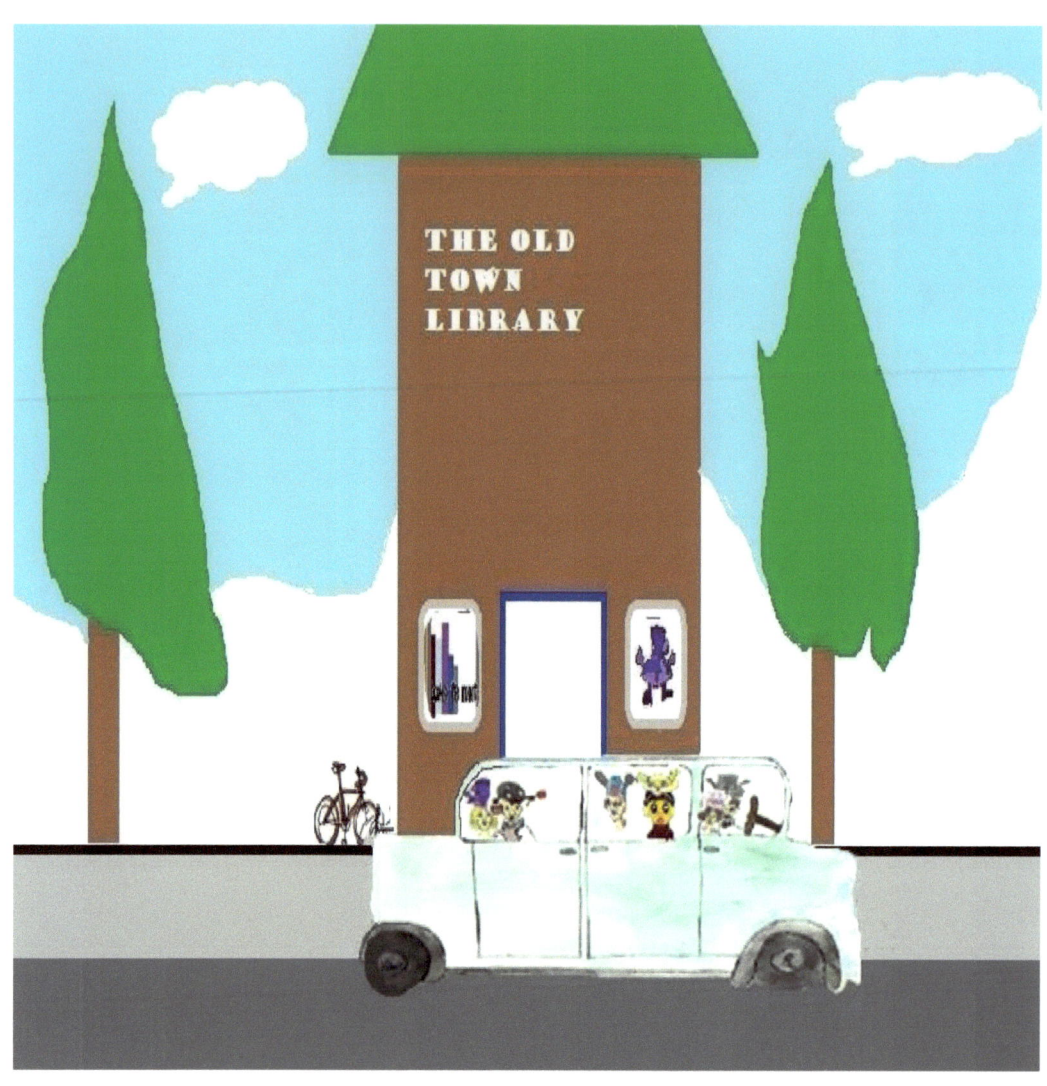

They pull up there was
VA-lay Parking

4

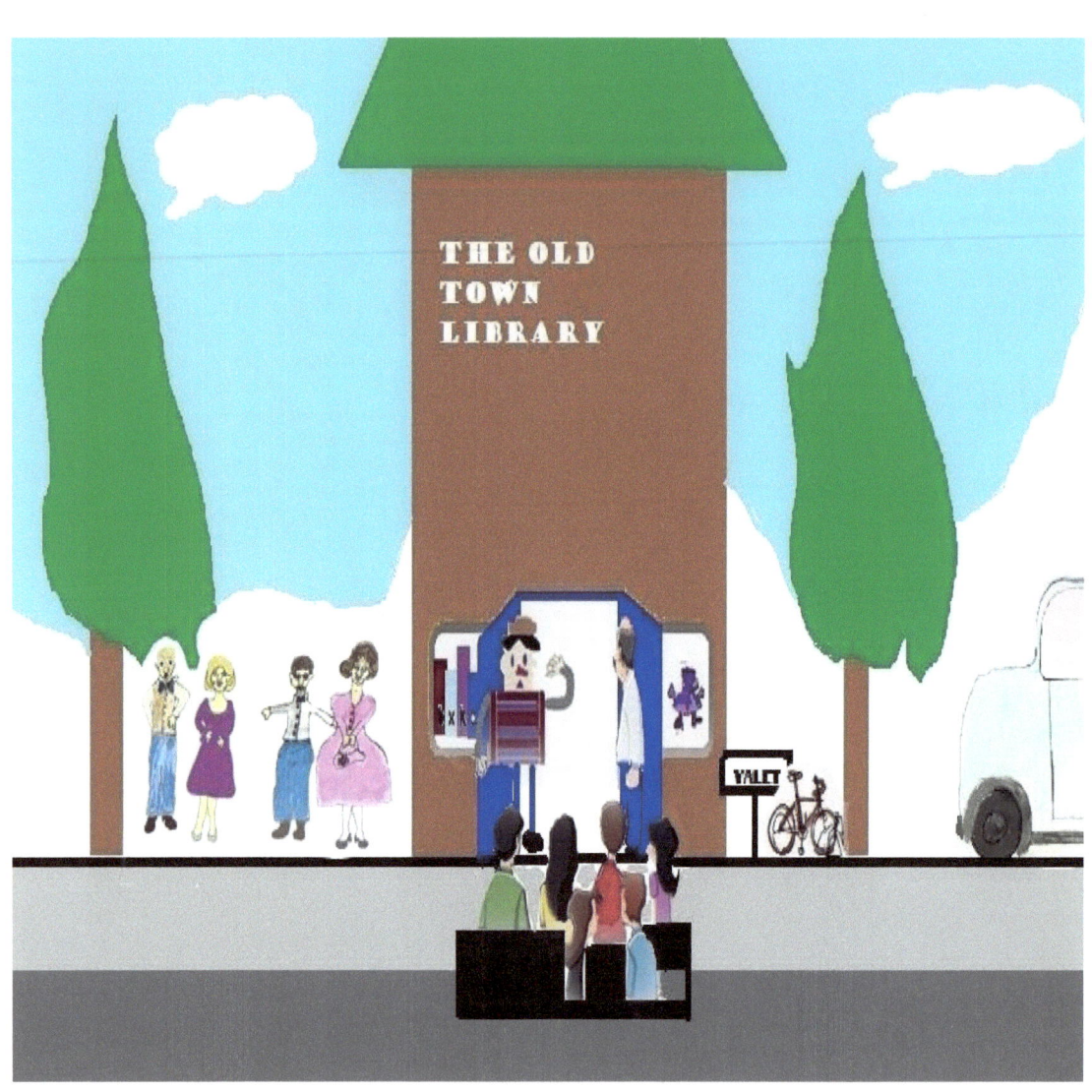

There was a big crewed out front and the mayor was there and he made a speech then the Librarian open the doors for all to come in there was cake and punch

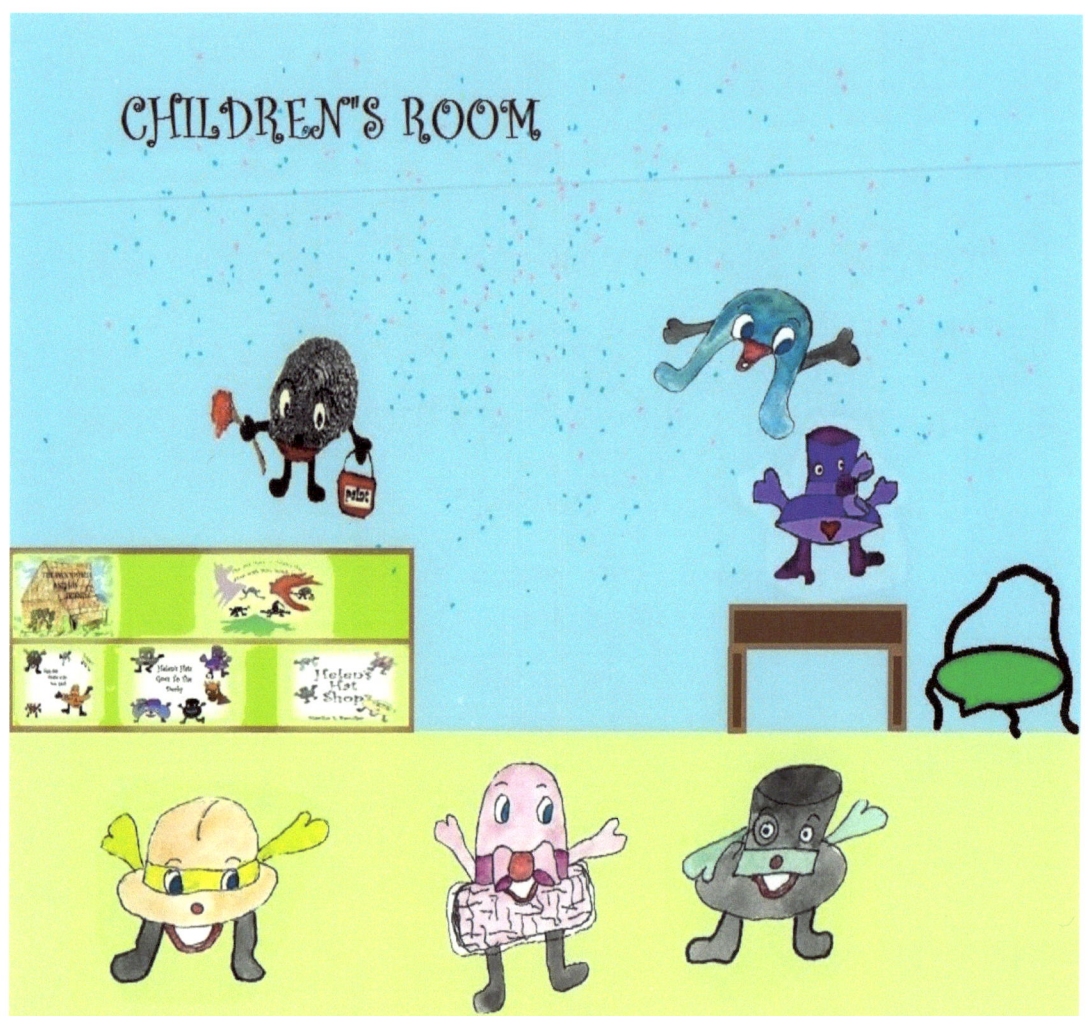

The Hat got all excited and jump off and went into the children room they were running all around the table

then they see the book on the a shelf

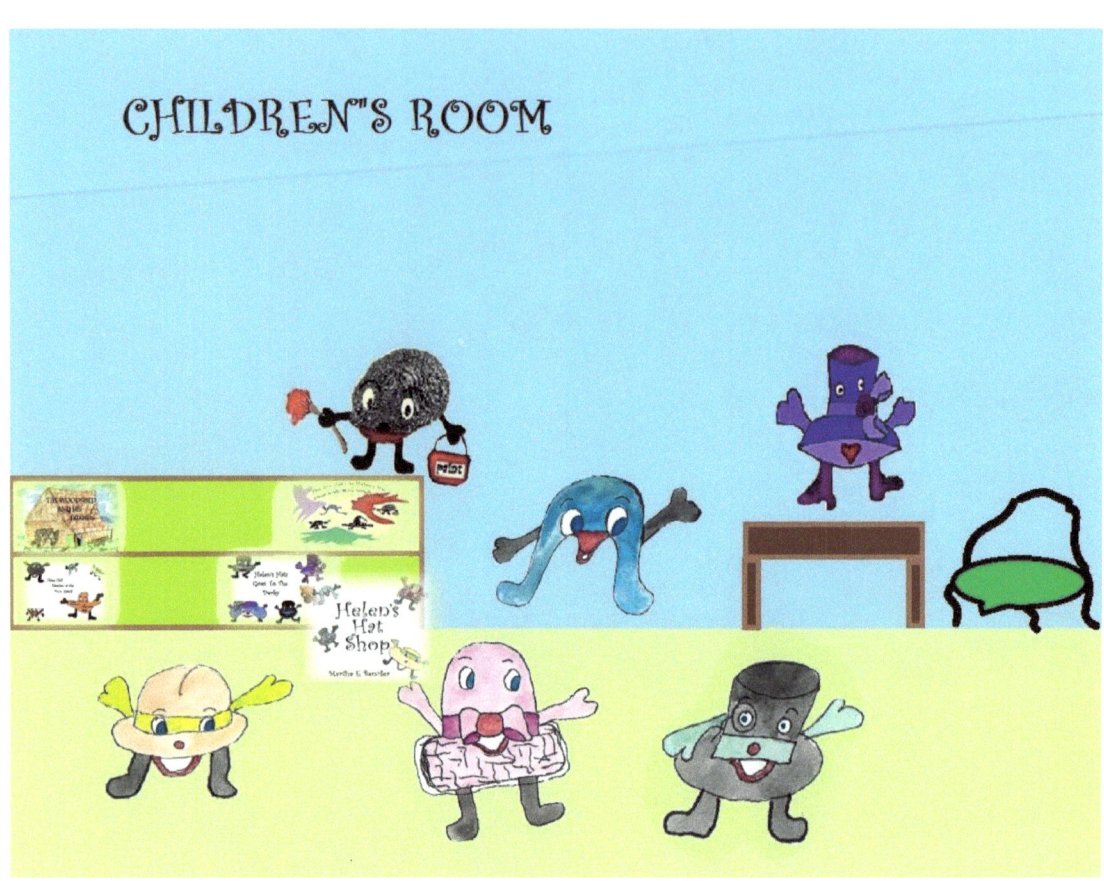

Miss. Pillbox see a book that had Hats on it and she said too the other it's a Hat book it us on the book cover.

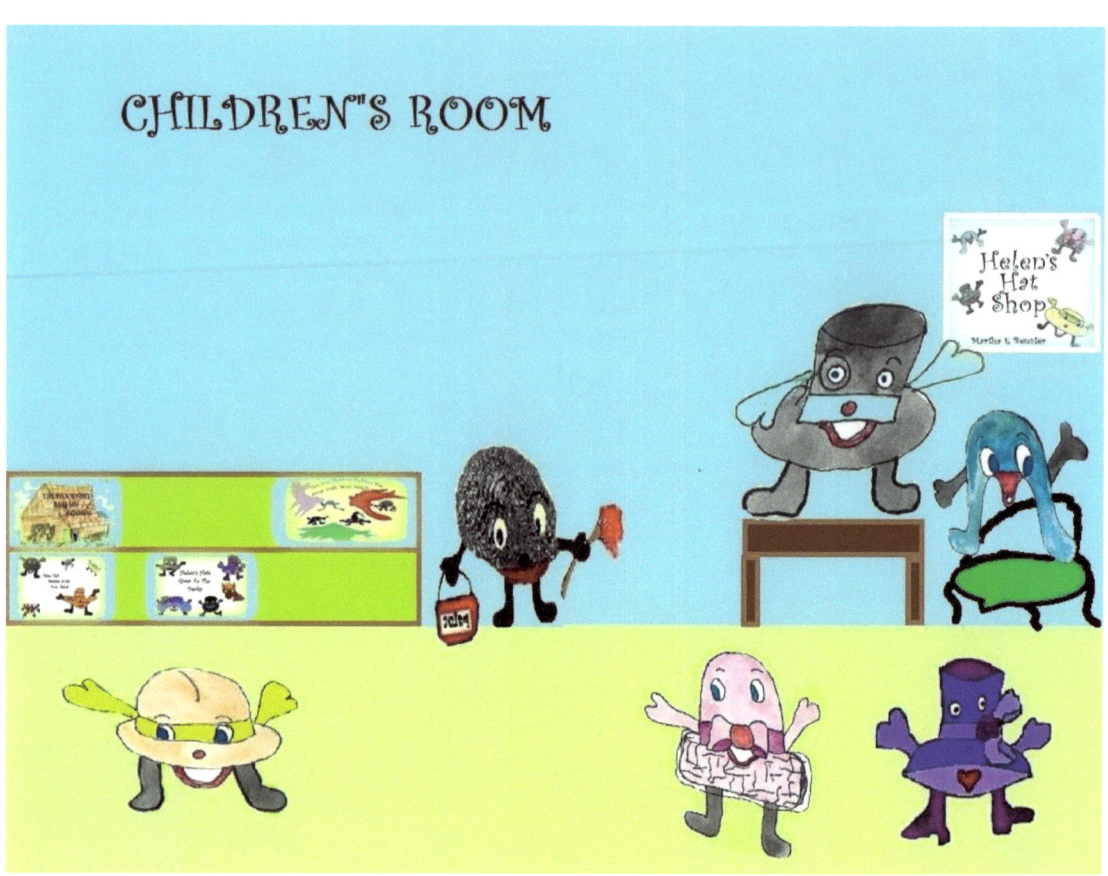

"Mr. Top Hat was the only one that could read." So they all where listing to him read
Helen's Hat Shop

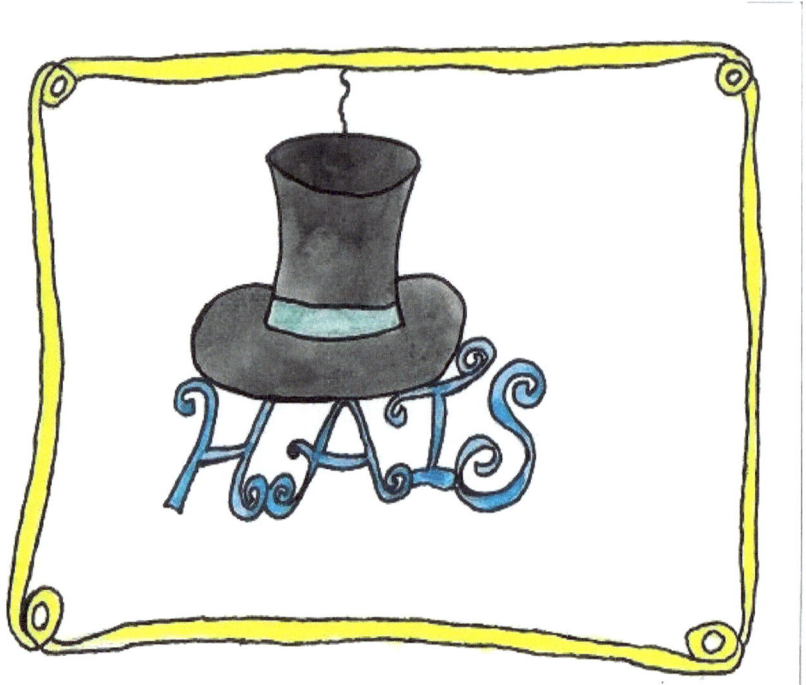

Helen closes the shop at five at night and leaves the florescent light on in the front window. It says Hat's. .And there's enough light to see inside the shop at night.

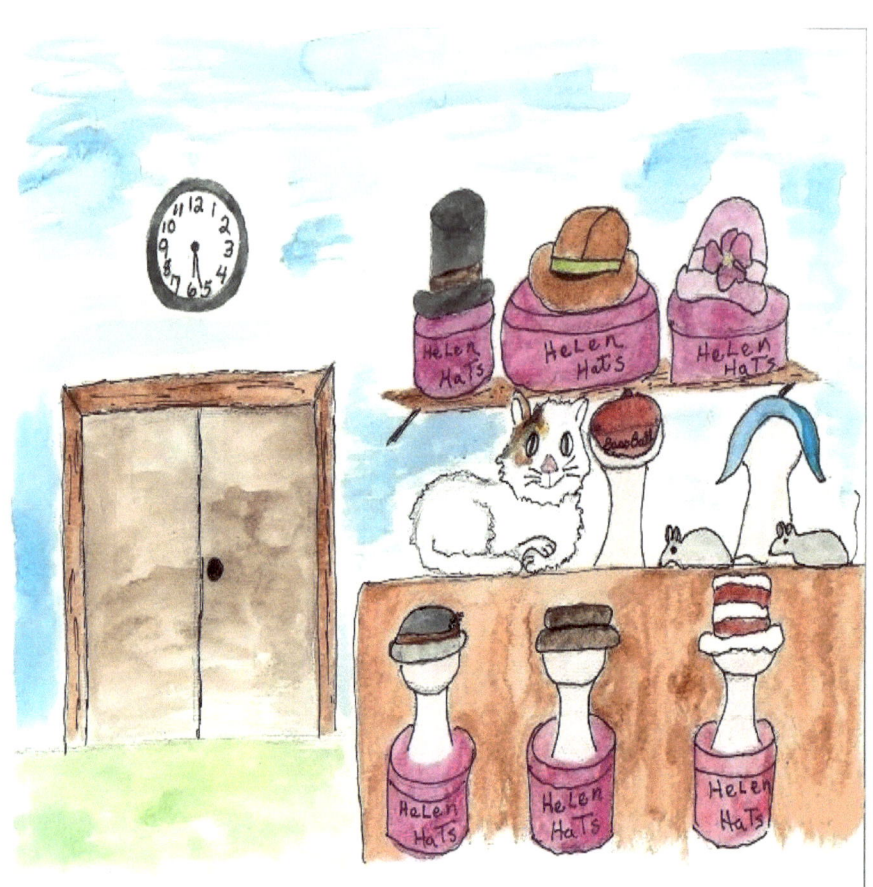

Mary, the cat that lives in the shop. like to come out at night, Too she likes to chase after the rats that Live with her there.

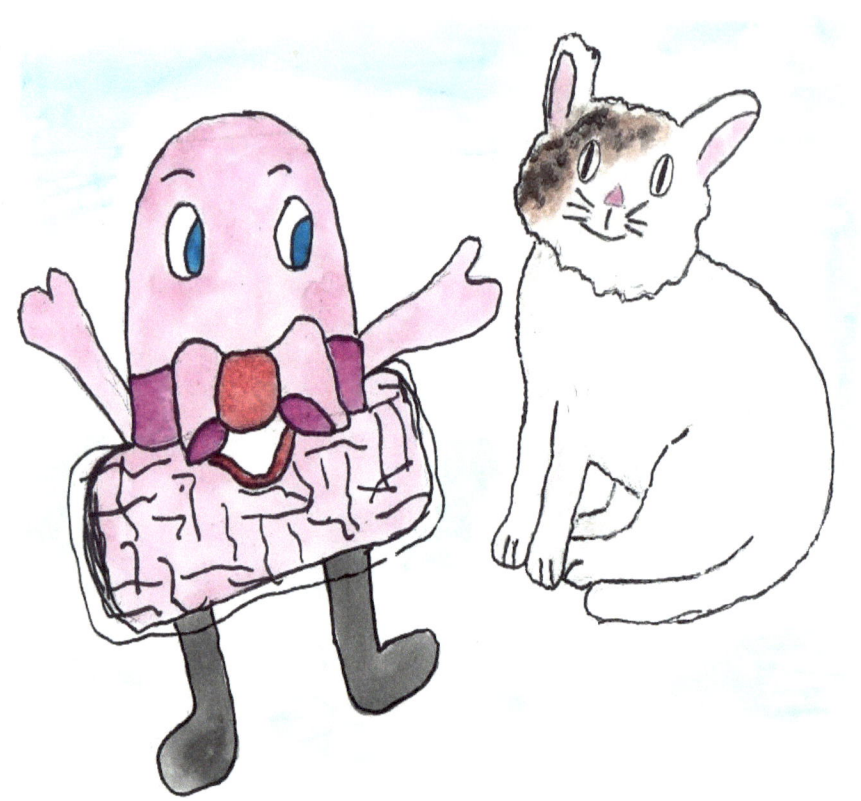

Mary the cat saw the hats running around and asked Miss Pillbox if they could all talk Miss Pillbox said yes, Why we can talk! You talk, don't you? Is that not true?" And Mary said "well yes, that's true."

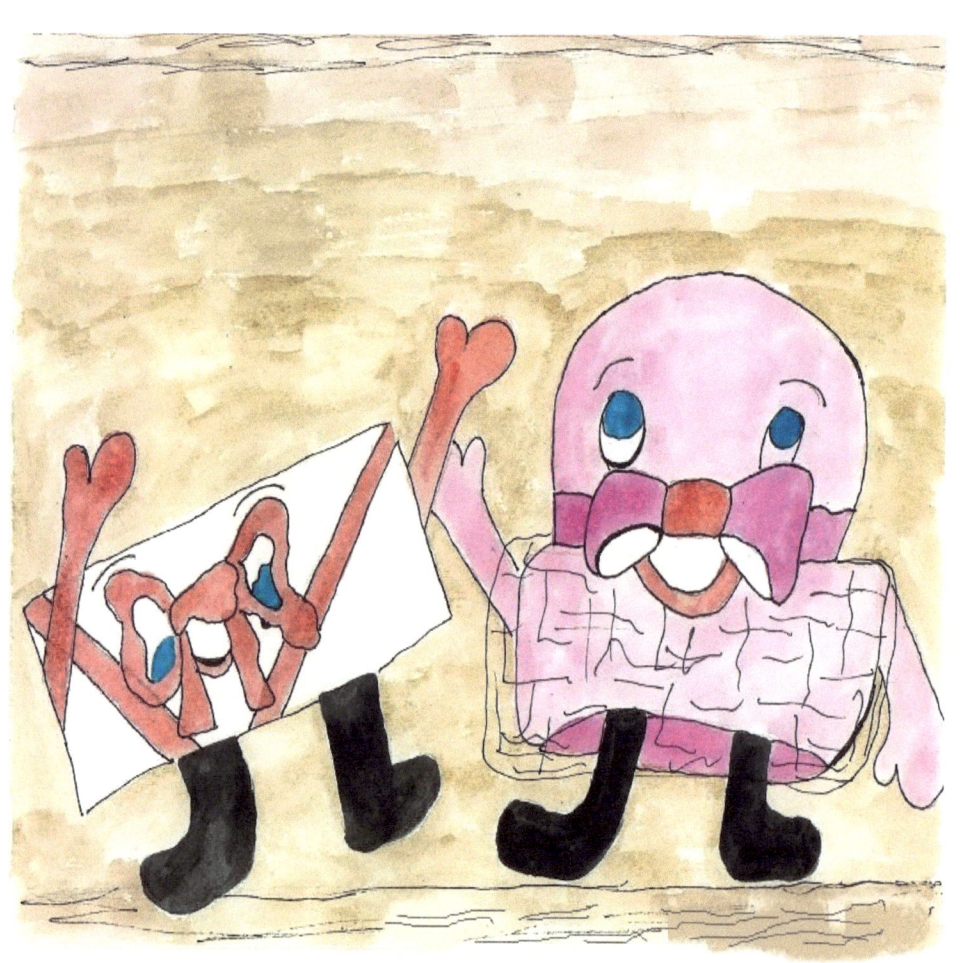

The hats were in the hat closet, and Miss Pillbox asked, "What is this place?" Miss. Box Hat said, "Its where we stay most of the time" Miss Pillbox did not like this closet it was small and dark inside. She asked Miss Box, "How do we get out and look around and have fun?"

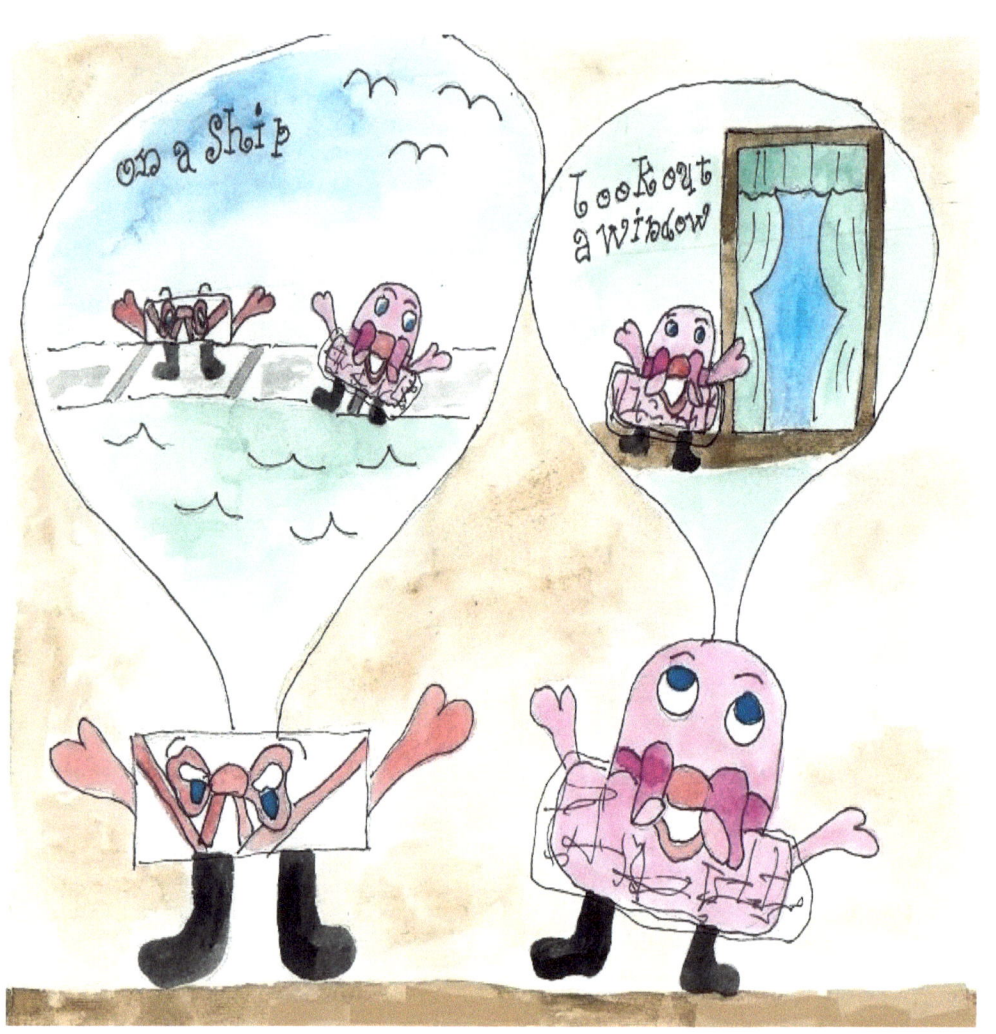

Miss. Box said, "Don't worry. It's fun when There's no one home on Sunday. So we get out and have a lot of fun. There are other times we taking on vacation on a big ship on the ocean. That's a lot of fun you wait and you wait and see!"

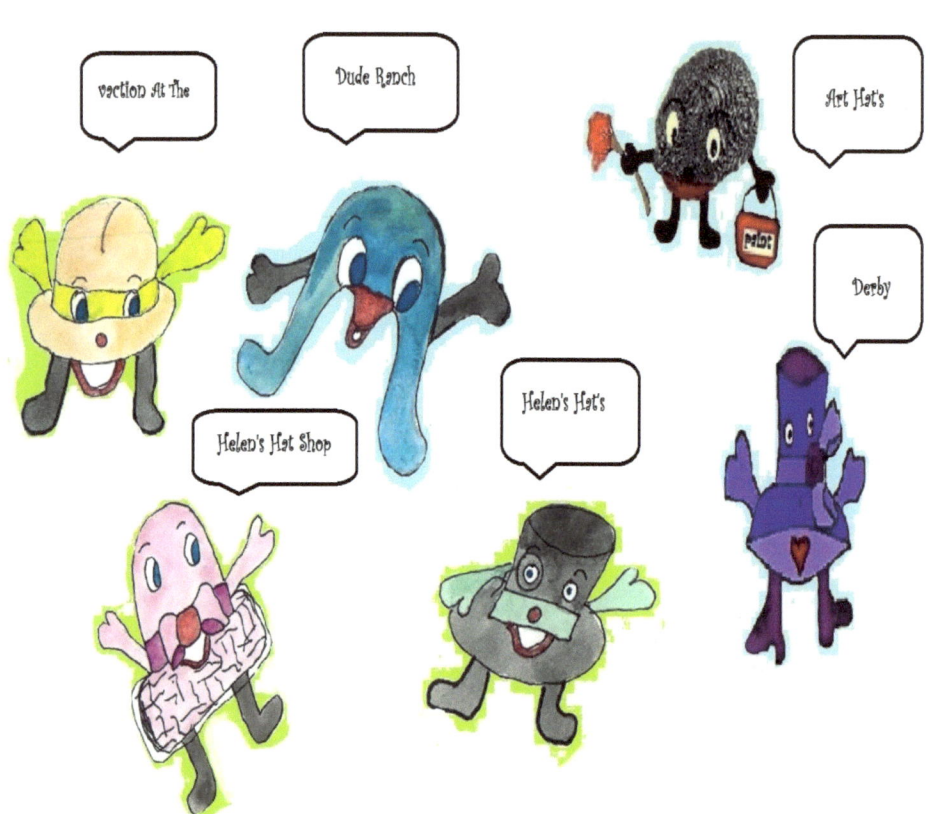

The book it was a lot of fun they did not remember doing the thing in the book there was four book. One was about the Hat Shop another the Derby and one is on a Vacation and The Art Hat's with Miss. Witch Hat

CHILDREN'S ROOM

The party was over and it was time to go home they all had a lot of fun Miss. Cloche said I hope we can come back some day Mr. Panama said we well the New Boy said I would like to paint the book in side and make them pretty

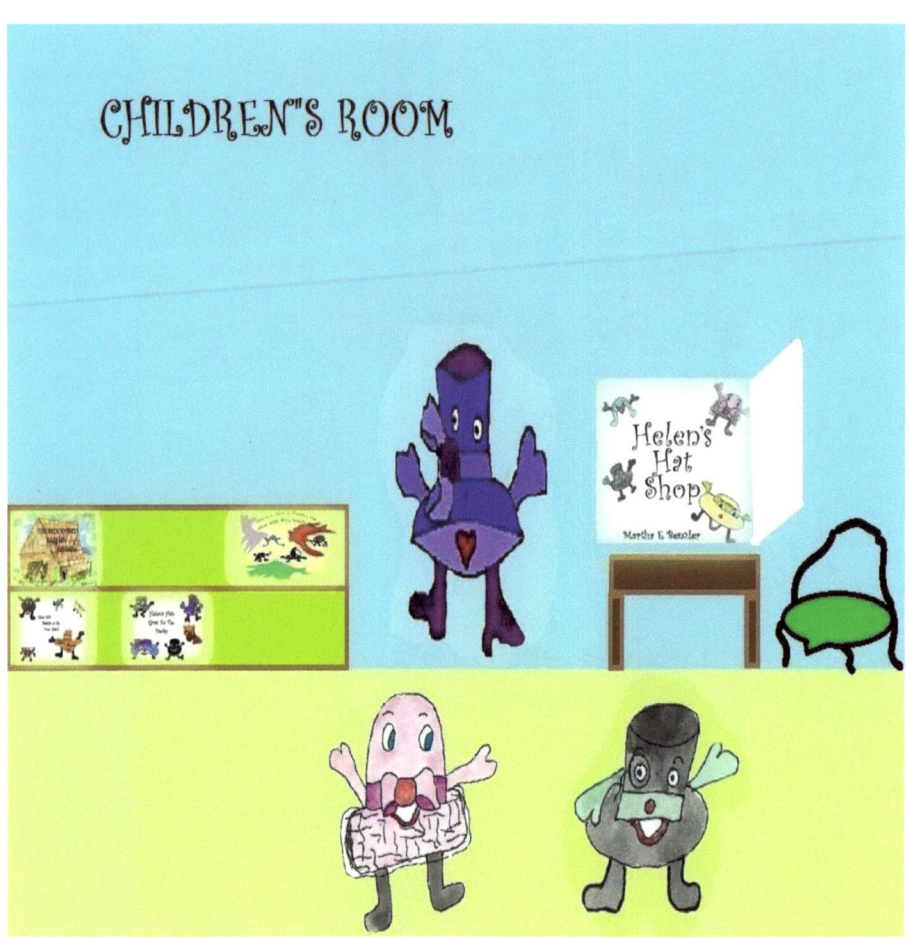

Mr. Top Hat and Miss. Pill Box and Missis laugh at them and said come on you silly Hats we well be left behind

THE END

www.ingramcontent.com/pod-product-compliance
Lightning Source LLC
Chambersburg PA
CBHW040451220526
45473CB00004B/1591